Super Stitches

A Book of Superstitions

Ann Nevins ▪ drawings by **Dan Nevins**

HOLIDAY HOUSE/NEW YORK

For the town of Indian Orchard

Library of Congress Cataloging in Publication Data

Nevins, Ann.
  Super stitches.

  Includes index.
  Summary: Explains the origins of such popular
beliefs and charms as the four-leaf clover, birthday
candles, Friday the thirteenth, three on a match,
knock on wood, rice at weddings, and groundhog's day.
  1. Superstition—Juvenile literature. [1. Superstition. 2. Charms] I. Nevins, Dan, ill. II. Title.
BF1775.N48 1983   398'.41   82-15875
ISBN 0-8234-0476-5

Contents

WHAT IS A SUPERSTITION?   5

GOOD LUCK   6

NUMBERS   17

BAD LUCK   21

EXPRESSIONS   33

WEDDINGS   44

WEATHER WARNINGS   52

OLD WIVES' TALES   55

INDEX   63

What Is a Superstition?

Do you ever knock on wood, cross your fingers, or carry a rabbit's foot for good luck? If you do, you are superstitious. But you aren't alone. There are millions of people who are superstitious. They believe that things happen because of luck.

How did superstitions begin? Why did they begin? They began more than four thousand years ago, when people thought there were many gods. They saw spirits in the sun, fire, rain, birth, death ... in almost everything.

Because life was hard in ancient times, people thought there were more bad spirits than good ones. To protect themselves, they invented charms and tricks to scare away the bad spirits. These charms and tricks, as well as other early beliefs, have come down to us through many generations. This book tells the origins of some of our most popular superstitions.

Good Luck

Cross

Few symbols have been used as much as the cross. It is found almost everywhere in the world. It was used in ancient South America, Mexico, Egypt, Greece, and China. In Scandinavian folklore, Thor, the god of thunder, had a hammer shaped like a cross. Christians think the cross is holy because Christ died on one almost two thousand years ago.

A scarecrow is shaped like a cross. Originally, a scarecrow was a cross that farmers planted in the ground to guard cornfields against evil spirits. Later, clothes were added to the cross to disguise it. Nowadays, farmers believe a scarecrow will keep away birds since it looks like a person.

Cross Your Fingers

Crossing your fingers on one hand when you make a wish is supposed to bring good luck. The wish is said to be trapped where the fingers meet. This custom comes from early Christians who thought a cross scared away the devil.

Four-Leaf Clover

Perhaps the four-leaf clover is considered lucky because it looks like a Christian cross. But the belief that it's lucky dates back to more than five thousand years ago—to long before the time of the Christians. The pre-Christians had a sun cross or solar cross. Using the sun as a guide, they painted pictures, showing a line between sunrise and sunset (or from east to west) and a line from north to south. Where these lines crossed formed a solar cross. Later, the four leaves of a clover became known as north, south, east, and west.

In ancient England, the Druids, who were sun worshipers, thought that anyone who found a four-leaf clover received a special "light" from the sun. This special gift gave them the power to see witches and devils. If devils could be seen and therefore avoided, this would bring good luck.

Horseshoe

In ancient times, people thought the new moon protected them from evil. They thought the horseshoe looked like the new moon. The Greeks, who invented the horseshoe, believed that the iron and seven nails used to shod a hoof kept people safe from witches and other evil things.

Today, hanging up a horseshoe is said to bring good luck.

Rabbit's Foot

Carry a rabbit's foot, and you might have good luck!
Ancient people believed that when rabbits thumped
the ground with their back feet, they "spoke." They
noticed also that when rabbits ran swiftly, their hind
feet touched the ground in front of their forefeet.
These strange facts made them think that the rear
feet held strong charms against evil.

The rabbit lives underground, yet no harm comes
to it from the evil spirits who some say lurk there.
And the rabbit has a great number of young. This fact
has led lots of people to think that if they wear a part
of the rabbit, they too will be charmed and have many
children.

Wish on a Wishbone

As long ago as three hundred years before Christ, the Etruscans, the early settlers of Italy, thought the hen and the rooster were special birds. Since a hen clucked when she laid an egg and a cock crowed each morning, the Etruscans believed the birds were messengers from the gods. A chicken was killed as a gift to a special god. Its collarbone was then saved and hung to dry.

Later, two people making separate wishes snapped the bone. The one with the longer piece got his wish. The one with the shorter piece got married first.

Wear Clothes Inside Out

Wearing clothes inside out all day is supposed to bring good luck. Many years ago, people did this to disguise themselves from the spirit of death. By hiding themselves in this way, they believed they could be saved from dying.

Salt over the Left Shoulder

At one time people used salt to keep their food from spoiling. However, in some places salt could not be found easily. Because it was rare and much needed, spilling salt was a sign that evil spirits were near. People believed that good spirits lived on the right side of the body and that evil spirits lived on the left side. To protect themselves from bad luck, people threw a pinch of salt over their left shoulder to bribe the demons. Some thought the demons would be blinded if the salt landed in their eyes.

Carry a Coin for Luck

A coin with a hole in it is an extra lucky charm. This belief began long before money was made. People thought that a stone or shell with a hole in it had been worn by some great god of the ocean. Wearing one around the neck would keep away evil and protect a person from drowning. Later, when money came into use, the belief was switched to coins.

Silver coins are said to scare away evil spirits. Silver, a symbol of the moon, is thought to bring health and wealth.

Birthday Candles

Years ago people lit bonfires to protect themselves from cold, darkness, evil spirits, and wild animals. Once the need for fire was gone, candles were lit as symbols of protection.

The ancient Greeks and Romans thought that candles had magical powers. They made wishes and offered prayers for the candle flames to "carry" to the gods.

Later, the Germans placed lighted candles on birthday cakes. They thought the candlelight would chase away evil spirits so that the day would be a happy one.

Today, a person makes a wish before blowing out the candles. The wish is supposed to be granted if all the candles are blown out with one puff.

Numbers

Unlucky Thirteen

Some say the Hindus of India were the first to believe that thirteen people sitting together was unlucky. However, this superstition probably comes from an old Scandinavian story about Loki, a well-known troublemaker. Loki was not invited to join twelve gods at a feast. Angry at being neglected, he went anyway. Later, he persuaded Hoder, a blind god, to shoot Balder, the god of goodness, with an arrow made of mistletoe. From that time on, people thought that thirteen at a table meant bad luck, and that someone sitting at the table would die within a year. People who are superstitious also give the Last Supper as an example of how thirteen people at a table caused bad luck; Christ died on the cross the following day.

There's a custom that if thirteen people stand up and hold hands, bad luck will not happen.

Lucky Seven

To the Egyptians, the number three was sacred. The three sides of a triangle stood for mother, father and son. The four sides of a square stood for the four directions: north, south, east, and west. By adding the three sides of the triangle to the four sides of a rectangle, the Egyptians made seven a lucky number. All through history seven turns up: seven seas, seven sins, seven graces, seven heavens, seven days of creation, seven plagues and so on.

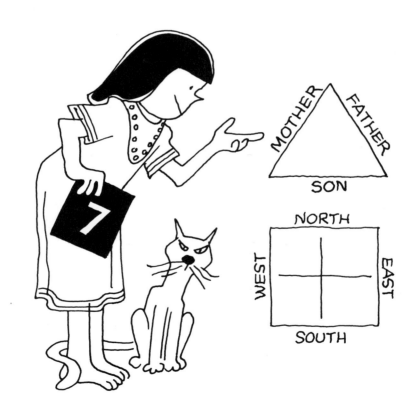

Lucky Four

Among the native American Indians, the number four was sacred. The Indians used it in special dances and also sang songs in groups of four.

In the Old Testament, four appears often: the four winds of Heaven, the four horns (the four men who succeeded Alexander the Great), and the four faces and the four wings in the prophet Ezekiel's vision. (Ezekiel mentions seeing four living creatures, each with "four faces and four wings.") In the New Testament, there are the four gospels written by Matthew, Mark, Luke, and John.

Bad Luck

Friday the 13th

People are supposed to have bad luck on Friday the 13th. Perhaps this is because Friday and the number thirteen have had a terrible history. Some people believe Eve tempted Adam with the apple on a Friday. Another myth says that the devil held a meeting with twelve witches on a Friday. Some also say that Christ died on the cross on a Friday and that the flood in the Bible took place on a Friday. All of these things suggest that Friday and the number thirteen must bring bad luck.

Tripping Is Bad Luck

There are many superstitions about tripping: "Don't trip at the beginning of the day or the day will be a bad one" or "Never stumble over the threshold of someone else's house." During World War II, it was a sign of bad luck if a soldier stumbled as he went into battle. If an actor or actress stumbles when he or she first walks on stage, it is an evil sign.

Some people think if you snap your fingers, you will scare away the evil spirit who made you stumble and good luck will return.

A Black Cat Crosses Your Path

If a black cat crosses your path, it means bad luck. This is a popular superstition. The Egyptians thought black cats were sacred. But in France, Germany, and parts of the United States, black cats were thought to be evil. It was believed that these cats were the friends of witches and brought bad luck.

If you really believe that black cats bring bad luck, this is what you do: take your hat off (if you're wearing one), turn it front to back on your head, and walk nine steps before turning your hat around again. This will ward off the evil spirits.

Break a Mirror, Seven Years of Bad Luck

Long before mirrors were made, a person was puzzled when he saw his face on the surface of a quiet pond. He thought that the image he saw must be his soul. When a breeze rippled the water and wrecked his image, he was sure evil would come his way. Later, he felt the same way when a mirror broke, because it once held his image.

By the first century, the Romans had added the idea that breaking a mirror would bring seven years of bad health. They thought that every seven years, life was made new again. Since the mirror held a person's image, a broken mirror meant seven years of poor health. Over the years, it came to mean seven years of bad luck instead of seven years of poor health.

Bad Luck to Open an Umbrella in the House

This superstition comes from Europe. Early rain umbrellas opened clumsily. If people weren't careful, the umbrella opened suddenly and often hit someone or broke something.

This superstition might also come from the beliefs of ancient sun worshipers. They thought umbrellas, or sun shades, were connected to the sun. Opening an umbrella indoors, away from the sun's rays, was an insult to the sun spirit. This brought bad luck too.

Wrong Side of the Bed

If you're grouchy in the morning, people sometimes say it's because you got up on the wrong side of bed. The right side of an object used to be its good side, and the left side, its evil or wrong side. That's why climbing out of bed on the left side was considered unlucky. If you got up on the wrong side, you had to walk backwards into the bed and get up again on the right side. If you didn't do this, you were supposed to have bad luck the whole day.

Kill an Albatross

It is considered bad luck to kill an albatross. Sailors tell many stories about this large seabird. One such story is that the albatross is the spirit of a drowned sailor who follows the ship to be with his shipmates. Another belief is that the albatross lifts shipwrecked sailors out of the ocean. In either case, some sailors say you should not kill this bird.

Three on a Match Is Unlucky

During the Boer War in Africa more than eighty years
ago, Tommies (the nickname for British soldiers)
found it unlucky to keep a match lit long enough to
light three cigarettes. "Three on a match" meant
death to one of the three soldiers. A match lit this
long made it possible for a sharpshooting Boer to see
enough to kill one of the men.

Break a Chain Letter

A chain letter promises good luck. It works this way: you receive a letter, which tells you to mail out a copy to a certain number of friends. They in turn must also send out a copy of the letter to their friends. If the "chain" is broken by anyone, that person will meet with bad luck. On the other hand, if everything is done right, good fortune will follow.

An American soldier in World War I was said to have begun this superstition. He believed that anyone carrying a chain letter would be saved from death, wounds, or capture. During World War II, chain letters were also very popular.

Nowadays, there is a law forbidding chain letters.

Turn a Photograph Over

Perhaps when you've been angry, you've turned over a picture of someone. There were people in the olden days who thought that this would cause bad luck.

In the 1700s, a man sometimes stared into a mirror for a long time. He hoped it would freeze his image so that it wouldn't go away. Then he'd give the mirror to a maiden he wanted to marry. If the lady liked him, she'd smile at the mirror. If she didn't like him, she'd turn the mirror over.

Walk under a Ladder

No doubt it was the ancient Egyptians who believed that evil spirits would punish anyone who walked under a ladder. This was because they thought the triangle was the sacred symbol of life, and a ladder forms a triangle when it leans against a wall. If someone walked under a ladder, he broke the triangle and upset the sacred symbol. Bad luck was sure to follow.

Expressions

Abracadabra

This word, spoken or written, was probably an ancient charm used to cure sickness. Some scholars say the Egyptians used it thousands of years ago. Others say it came from the ancient Hebrew words *b'rachá* (blessing) and *davár* (word). In any case, it had to be written down like an upside-down triangle. As mentioned before, the triangle was the Egyptian symbol for life. When *Abracadabra* was spoken out loud or written down, it was supposed to cure toothaches, cramps, fevers, and other illnesses.

Cross My Heart, Hope to Die

The saying "Cross my heart and hope to die" is supposed to prove you are telling the truth. While saying the words, you trace a large cross (a religious cross) over your heart. Many years ago, our ancestors believed that the cross was a symbol of good luck and that the heart was the root of wisdom. It was believed that if a person lied, while placing a cross over his heart, death would be sure to follow.

Lucky at Cards, Unlucky at Love

Cards and love go hand in hand. You take a chance
when you play cards. You take a chance when you fall
in love. Both depend on luck for success. Most people
believe that luck doesn't work two ways at once.
Therefore, if you're lucky at cards, you must be unlucky at love.

Knock on Wood

In folklore, trees are the homes often of friendly gods. These gods make the trees change with the seasons, or stay "evergreen" all year around.

The ancient Druids of England thought the oak tree was sacred. They believed it had the power to heal or bring harm. If a person wanted to ask a favor of the tree god, he or she touched the bark.

Some ancient Europeans also believed that knocking on wood kept jealous evil spirits from hearing good news. The wood-touching rite gained extra strength when Christ died on a wooden cross.

Today, in order to prevent bad luck from happening, many people knock on wood after boasting or speaking of good fortune.

Dimple on the Chin, Devil Within

A dimple in your cheek,
Many hearts you will seek;
A dimple in your chin,
Many hearts you will win.

A dimple in your cheek,
You are gentle, mild and meek;
A dimple in your chin,
You have a devil within.

People with dimples are supposed to like having fun. But some say they have bad tempers and like to make mischief. At one time, people who had dimples were thought to have powers of good and evil. Today, dimples are a mark of beauty.

Dimples are caused really by skin sticking to deeper tissue.

Heads You Win, Tails You Lose

The ancient Romans liked to flip coins for fun. The head of Julius Caesar, their ruler, was on one side of a coin. When the side with his head came up, the person who flipped the coin was said to have the power of Caesar behind him. It was the winning side. The other side of the coin—the losing side—was called a tail.

Company Is Coming

Drop a spoon,
Company soon.
Knife falls,
Gentleman calls.
Fork falls,
Lady calls.
Spoon falls,
Baby calls.

Dropping silverware on the floor can mean that company is coming. If a fork is dropped, a female might visit. If a knife is dropped, a male might visit. In some parts of the world, the meanings are the opposite. These symbols have existed for centuries.

Achoo! God Bless You!

Early Christians thought that their breath and soul were the same thing. When they sneezed, they believed their soul escaped from their body unless they asked God to prevent it. They borrowed this custom from non-Christians who asked their gods for protection in the same way.

During the Middle Ages, the Germans thought that evil spirits entered the body through the nostrils and ears when someone sneezed. To get rid of these spirits, a person had to sneeze again, causing the spirits to travel from body to body. Nowadays, we know that sneezing spreads cold germs, not evil spirits. Perhaps this is why the Germans say *Gesundheit,* or "Health," after they sneeze.

Star Light, Star Bright

The ancient Babylonians believed that their lives were run by the stars. Each person had his own "star of destiny" which directed the events of his life. If a person had an evil star, it caused bad luck. If he was born under a star of good fortune, only good things would happen.

If You Step on a Crack, You'll Break Your Mother's Back

Step in a hole,
You'll break your mother's sugar bowl,
Step on a crack
You'll break your mother's back . . .

It was once believed that a crack was an opening to a grave. If you stepped on a crack by mistake, some member of your family would die.

Weddings

Three Times a Bridesmaid, Never a Bride

This superstition comes from the belief "never two without three." If two bad events happened, a third was sure to follow. If you were a bridesmaid two times, your chances of getting married were slim indeed. This could be prevented if you were a bridesmaid seven times. The moon changed every seven days. So it was believed that if you were a bridesmaid seven times, your luck would change, just as the moon changed.

Ring on the Left Hand

The ring is worn on the left hand because the heart, the symbol of love, is on the left side. It's worn on the fourth finger because the Egyptians believed it held a vein running directly to the heart.

A June Wedding

Many couples like to get married in June. This comes from a Roman myth about Juno, the goddess of women. She was said to bless weddings that took place during her month.

Something Old, Something New, Something Borrowed, Something Blue

This custom seems to come from England. "Something old" is a piece of clothing, worn by the bride, that belonged to a happily married older woman. By wearing the clothing of the older woman, the bride hoped she too would have good fortune. "Something new" is generally a handkerchief. "Something borrowed" is usually a piece of golden jewelry. Witches do not like the color blue, because it is the color of heaven. So the bride wears "something blue" to keep witches away.

Wedding Cake under a Pillow

If a female takes a piece of cake home from a wedding and places it under her pillow, she's supposed to dream about the man she will marry. This superstition probably started with the Romans. A cake was broken over the bride's head as a symbol of wealth and as a wish for her to have children. The guests then picked up the pieces so that they could enjoy the good luck themselves.

Throw Rice at Weddings

People threw rice at the bride and groom in ancient Hindu and Chinese weddings because they thought the couple would then have many children. The throwing and eating of rice or other grains was also a symbol of wealth, health, and happiness. There is another very old superstition that during a marriage ceremony, evil spirits lurk near the wedding couple. Throwing rice or grain is supposed to feed them and keep them away from the bride and groom.

Tie an Old Shoe to the Bride and Groom's Car

An old shoe used to stand for power, ownership, and good luck. In Scotland and Ireland, the shoe was not only thrown with good wishes at newlyweds, but at anyone starting something new. There was a time when the father of the bride gave her old shoes to the new husband. This was a sign that the husband must now take care of her. Sometimes, the new husband would hit his bride on the head with a shoe to show her who was boss.

Weather Warnings

Groundhog's Day

The groundhog is supposed to leave his hole on February 2 to check the weather. If he sees his shadow in the sun, there will be six more weeks of winter. If it is cloudy and he can't see his shadow, then spring is on its way. This superstition comes from Europe where the hedgehog, a small animal with stiff spines, checks the weather on February 2. Since the early colonists did not find hedgehogs in America, they chose the groundhog to tell the weather for them.

In like a Lion, Out like a Lamb

Many people think the weather for each month will be decided by the weather on the month's first few days. Perhaps this is where the saying about the month of March—"In like a lion, out like a lamb"— comes from. If it is windy and "roars like a lion" at the beginning of March, then it will be gentle like a lamb at the end.

Old Wives' Tales

Stork Brings a Baby

A stork is a faithful mate all during its life. The ancient Romans thought so much of the stork that they named a law after it. It was called "The Stork Law," and it meant that adult children had to take care of their aged parents. The legend that "the stork brings a baby" probably got started because the stork is such a well-liked bird.

Cutting Hair Causes Weakness

No doubt this belief comes from the Bible story about Samson and Delilah. The story is about how Samson lost his strength when his hair was cut by Delilah. Also, there was an ancient European belief that hair was like the sun's rays. Since the sun shone for fewer hours during the winter months, people thought the sun lost its strength. So it seemed to follow that cutting someone's hair would leave that person weak.

Redheads Have Bad Tempers

Most of our ancestors thought the color red meant fire. If you had red hair, then you were said to have a fiery nature or a bad temper. Egyptians, Greeks, and Romans thought redheads were unlucky. During the Middle Ages, many redheads were burned at the stake as witches.

Left-Handers Are Clumsy

The ancient Romans called the left side the "sinister" side. To them it meant left-handers were evil and could not be trusted.

Because most people are right-handed, they sometimes think left-handers are strange and clumsy. Teachers used to even make left-handers learn to write with their right hands.

Itching or Burning Ears

If your right ear itches or burns, someone is supposed to be speaking about you in a nice way. However, if your left ear itches, someone is speaking poorly of you. In Holland, to "get back" at the person speaking poorly of you, people bite the little finger of the left hand. This is said to cause the person who is speaking badly of you to bite his or her tongue.

Rats Desert a Sinking Ship

Rats and men leave a sinking ship. In earlier days, sailors believed that rats seemed to know beforehand if a ship was about to sink. Probably the real reason they left is because they often chewed holes in the side of the ship. When the water rushed in, they were the first to see it and leave.

Cats Have Nine Lives

The ancient Egyptians saw that cats survived many
bad falls. Because of this, they believed the cat lived
more than once. They connected the cat with the
number three, which stood for mother, father, and
son. The idea behind the number three was that the
life cycle (mother, father, and son) went on from generation to generation. When a cat survived a fall, its
life went on too.

Among the Egyptians, the number three was powerful and when it was doubled and became six and tri-
pled and became nine, it was a more powerful number
still. Nine was the most respected number granted to
anything. So with this in mind, the cat was given nine
lives.

Index

Abracadabra, 34
Albatross, 28
American Indians, 20

Bad luck, 21–32, 36
Bed, wrong side, 27
Bible, 20, 22, 57
Black cat, 24
Blue (color, 48

Cards, luck at, 36
Cats, black, 24; nine lives,
    62
Chain letters, 30
Charms, 5, 11, 15
Christians, 7–9, 18, 22, 41
Clothes, wearing inside out,
    13
Coin, flipping, 39; lucky, 15
Cracks, 13
Cross, 7, 9
"Cross my heart", 35
Crossed fingers, 8

Dimples, 38
Druids, 9, 37

Ears, itching or burning, 60
Egyptians, 19, 32, 34, 46,
    58, 62
Etruscans, 12
Expressions, 33–43
Ezekiel, 20

Fingers, crossed, 8; snap-
    ping, 23

Four (number), 20
Four-leaf clover, 9
Friday the 13th, 22

Good luck, 6–16
Greeks, 19, 58
Groundhog's day, 53

Haircutting, 57
Handkerchief, 48
Heart, 35, 46
Hedgehog, 53
Horseshoe, 10

June wedding, 47

"Knock on wood", 37

Ladder, walking under, 32
Left hand, ring on, 46
Left-hand persons, 59
Luck, bad, 21–32; good,
    6–16
"Lucky at cards", 36
Lucky charms, coin, 15;
    rabbits foot, 11
Lucky expressions, 33–34

March weather, 54
Match, three on one light,
    29
Mirrors, 31; breaking, 25
Moon, 10

Nine (number), 62
Numbers, 17–20, 22, 25, 62

Old shoes, 51
Old wives' tales, 55–62

Photographs (pictures),
    turning over, 31

Rabbit's foot, 11
Rats, 61
Red hair, 58
Rice (at weddings), 50
Ring (on left hand), 46
Romans, 25, 39, 47, 49, 56,
    58

Salt (over shoulder), 14
Sayings (expressions),
    33–43
Scarecrows, 7
Seven (number), 19, 25
Sidewalk cracks, 43
Silver, 15
Silverware, dropping, 40
Sinking ship, 61

Sneezing, 41
Solar cross, 9
Square and rectangle, 19
Stars, 42
Stork (bringing baby), 56
Sun, 9, 26
Superstitions, 5

Thirteen (number), 18,
    22
Thor (god), 7
Three (number), 45, 62
Trees, 37
Triangle, 19, 32, 34
Tripping, 23

Umbrella (opening in
    house), 26

Weather warnings, 52–54
Wedding, 44–51; cake, 49
Wishbones, 12
Wood, 37